100 IDEAS FOR MAKING PROFITABLE NICHE PRODUCTS

ANNABELLE JEFFREY

ISBN: 9798355353377

DEDICATION

This book is dedicated to all of my students, even those who have not yet discovered my contents.

"DISCLAIMER"

Not Liable

In no event will the product's designer, programmer, distributor(s), or any distributor(s) be liable to any party for any direct, indirect, punitive, special, incidental, or any consequential damages arising directly or indirectly from the use of this product. This item is given "as is" and without any guarantees.

By using this product, you agree to the "No Liability" policy. You are not allowed to use or distribute this product if you disagree with our "No Liability" policy (if applicable.)

If you choose to use this product, your failure to read this notice in its entirety will not change your acceptance to this policy.

You might not be covered by the aforementioned limitation or exclusion because applicable law might not permit the exclusion or limitation of incidental or consequential damages.

Regardless of the legal action's format, the maximum amount of culpability for damages is limited to the real cost of the product.

1.Increasing Income - The majority of people desire to increase their income. They wish to keep from having to go without purchasing whatever they desire and need. You could concentrate on market segments for job, side hustles, affiliate marketing, career progression, etc.

2. Increasing Sales And Profits - Most companies aim to boost their revenue and profits. Marketing, copywriting, advertising, cost-cutting, publicity advice, etc. could all be your niche markets.

3.Choosing Wisely - The majority of investors desire high rates of return. You can choose to focus on market niches for products related to futures trading, bond investing, and stock market investing.

4. Getting A Raise – Employees want to keep their jobs and avoid being on a low pay range at their workplace. You may focus on market segments for products related to workplace communication, such as soliciting raises, getting hired, and so forth.

5.Getting Promoted - The majority of workers want to advance and give their employers their best. Product niches concerning climbing the corporate ladder, advancing your career, exceeding or falling short of expectations at work and the effects of each could be your focus.

6. Working from Home – Many people choose to work from home. You may concentrate on markets for products related to network marketing, affiliate marketing, starting a home business, and other related topics.

7.Working Less - Most people desire to work less but more intelligently. You could choose to focus on market segments for products related to enterprises that require little to no effort, automated revenue streams, part-time employment that pay the same as 40-hour work weeks, etc.

8.Eliminating Debt - Most people wish to keep their debt under control or eliminated. You may choose to target markets for products related to debt relief, money management, and preventing debt collection calls, among other topics.

9.Outstanding Credit - Everyone wants to have excellent credit. The improvement of their credit records, effective money management, raising their credit scores, etc., could be your specialty markets.

10.Stumbling Into A Deal - Most people enjoy stumbling upon deals. You can choose to target markets for goods that teach consumers how to be frugal, haggle for cheaper pricing, locate great deals, etc.

11.Retiring Early - The majority of people desire to retire early or to at least have sufficient funds for their golden years. You may focus on markets that deal with topics like setting goals, long-term investing, and early retirement planning.

12.Education - A lot of people desire to further their education. You may focus on markets for goods related to college grants, reviews, loans, and housing arrangements, among other topics.

13.Saving money is a goal shared by most people. You may concentrate on markets that deal with setting up a budget, paying off debt, stretching a person's budget farther, smart shopping, etc.

14. Being Successful - The majority of people aspire to succeed. Product niches centered on setting and achieving goals, using motivational strategies, adopting the proper frame of mind, etc., could be your focus.

15. Having Good Luck - Most individuals enjoy winning. You might concentrate on markets that deal with gambling, winning at games of chance, choosing winning numbers for the lottery, top hotels near casinos, etc.

16.Leading - Many people aspire to be in positions of leadership. You might focus on market segments for products related to leadership traits, interaction with followers, public education, etc.

17.Expertise - The majority of people aspire to the status of expert. Product niches related to study techniques, memory enhancement, brain power enhancement, taking initiative, etc. could be your focus.

18.Looking Credible - Many individuals want to project credibility. You might choose to target markets for products related to enhancing educational credentials, advancing your career, publicizing your abilities, making the headlines, etc.

19.Getting Information – People often try to avoid being in the dark about issues that can affect their way of life. You could choose to target markets for products related to publishing news, selling information, producing information products, information technology, etc.

20.Finding A Job - A lot of people need to comprehend their role in the workforce, such as how to obtain a position. How to conduct an interview effectively. You may choose to focus on markets for products related to job training, job listings, and resume writing. ETC

21.The majority of people strive to appear attractive to others. You could concentrate on markets for goods related to cosmetic surgery, hair care, dressing for success, and other topics.

22.Most individuals want to stay healthy, thus this is number 22. You might concentrate on markets for goods related to vitamins, healthy eating strategies, disease prevention, and nutritional supplements.

23.Living a long life is a goal shared by the majority of individuals. You could focus on markets for products related to nutrition, exercise, safe sex contraception, anti-aging drugs, medical exams, and other areas.

24.Having no pain - This is something that most people strive for. The newest medical research and treatments, pain-relieving workouts, non-prescription pain remedies, etc. are some examples of product niches you could target.

25.Being Physically Fit – Being physically fit is something that many people strive towards. You might concentrate on markets for products related to fitness routines, gear, videos, gym memberships, etc.

Additionally, you might form partnerships with businesses in the industry by providing incentives like discounts.

26, Having Plenty Of Energy – This is something that many individuals desire. You may focus on markets for items related to energizing foods, caffeine, sleep, energy drinks, and other topics.

27.Being drug-free is something that many individuals strive for, whether it be via legal or illicit means. You might concentrate on markets for products related to drug treatment and alternative remedies.

28.Having A Collection - The majority of people have some sort of collection. Products like dolls, plates, antique books, glassware, trading cards, coins, trinkets, and nick-knacks are a few examples of possible product niches.

29.Fame - A lot of people dream of achieving fame and popularity. You might concentrate on market segments that deal with topics like how to attract people to you, how to become well-known, etc.

30.Being Trendy and In Style - Many people aspire to be fashionable and trendy. You may concentrate on markets for products related to apparel, accessories, and information about fashion, among others.

31.Being in good mental health is something that many individuals strive towards. Insomnia, worry, limiting beliefs, and other negative feelings are things they wish to avoid. Self-help books, hypnotherapy, and mental therapy, among other things, could be your chosen product niches.

32.Be Smart/Intelligent – Many people want to be seen as smart or intelligent. You could focus on market segments such as rising IQs, boosting cognitive power, expanding vocabulary, raising grade averages, and education.

33.Being sociable is something that many individuals strive to do. You might focus on market segments for products like communication advice, communication technology, social gatherings, social events, and social skills, among others.

34.Being First - The majority of people aspire to be at the top of their field or in their profession. They have come to believe that planning ahead is preferable. Product themes like "first to know" knowledge, how to always be number one, developing good listening skills, etc. might be your focus.

35.Having No Risk - A lot of people try to steer clear of hazards in life. They stay away from risky situations since they might not be able to afford the results. You might focus on market segments for products like smoke detectors, safety gear, life insurance, legal insurance, and medical insurance.

36.Being in love or finding love is what most people aspire to. Along with that, they try to stay away from anything harmful. For example, divorcing, breaking up, etc. You might concentrate on specific market segments, such as relationship counseling, dating services, singles bars, etc.

37.Marriage is something that a lot of individuals want to do. You may choose to focus on pre-marital services and product niches like wedding attire, accessories, and supplies.

38.Attracting Men/Women - Most people wish to appear alluring to the other sex. You might concentrate on markets for products like sexy advice, makeovers, stylish clothing, fragrances, and colognes.

39.Saving Memories – Most people strive to preserve their memories and recollections. In order to preserve them and pass them down to their offspring, they wish to. You might focus on particular product niches like those for cameras, camcorders, photo albums, paintings, diaries, and journals, among others.

40.Most individuals aspire to be good parents, which brings us to number forty. Parenting manuals, parenting workshops, anger management programs, stress management, etc. are a few examples of possible product niches.

41.The majority of people find sex to be enjoyable. Products like contraception, how-to manuals, films, periodicals, tips on being romantic, dating services, etc. could be your focus.

42.Saving time is a common goal for most individuals. You might concentrate on market niches for products like daily planners, goods with immediate benefits like laundry services, meal planning and delivery, etc.

43.Achieving a Goal - Most people aspire to accomplish goals in their personal and professional lives. The goal setting information, motivational goods, hypnosis, seminars, etc. are a few examples of possible product niches to target.

44.Developing A Talent Or Skill - A lot of people wish to develop a talent or skill. Product niches including educational classes, at-home training, private instruction, how-to books and videos, etc., could be your focus.

45.Fulfilling a Craving - Especially when dieting, most people desire to satisfy a craving. They enjoy foods that taste rich or opulent without really adding fat. Product segments like low-fat, low-calorie, and sugar-free foods, among others, could be your focus.

46.Satisfying Hunger - People desire to satiate their appetites. You might provide a balanced overview of the options while focusing on specialist products like quick food services, food items, spices, instant foods, etc.

47.People seek to quench their thirst, which brings us to our next point. You could choose to focus on specialized goods like quick drink services, beverage items, mixes, instant drinks, portable drinks, etc.

48.Losing Weight – Losing weight is something that many people desire. You can choose to target specialized goods like low-carb foods, workout gear, low-fat desserts, hypnosis, diet regimens, and meal bars for dieters.

49.Realizing a Dream or Fantasy - Many people wish to realize a dream or fantasy. Choosing exotic holidays, examining pricey goods, developing strategies for reaching ambitions, etc. are a few examples of niche products you could focus on.

50.The majority of individuals desire cleanliness and sanitization. Products like antibacterial soaps, bath and shower accessories, hand sanitizer, etc. could be your specialized market.

51.The desire to be more structured is widespread. Schedulers, advice on organization, closet organizers, and other specialized products could be your focus.

52.The majority of people find the sensation of freedom to be enjoyable. To not feel constrained or constrained is what they seek. You may focus on specialty goods such as prospects for home businesses, real estate, an apartment locator service, travel arrangements, etc.

53.Getting Pleasure - Most people would choose pleasure than pain or anguish. The use of massage therapy, painkillers, trip arrangements, and other specialized goods and services could be your niche market.

54.The majority of people wish to get through their hurdles. You might concentrate on providing specialized goods and services like motivating audios, subliminal goal reminders, and assistance with overcoming limiting beliefs.

55.Owning valuable and uncommon items is a common desire among humans. You might concentrate on specialized goods and services like those related to diamonds, antiques, collectibles, etc.

56. Being Entertained - The majority of people seek entertainment. You might focus on specialized goods like humor, music, TV series, books, DVDs, live performances, etc.

57.Most individuals want to stay out of trouble or, if they are already in it, to find some relief. You might concentrate on certain niche markets for things like legal goods, legal insurance, legal knowledge, avoiding social pressure, etc.

58.Having Friends - The majority of people desire friends. You might market specialized goods such as hangouts for nice people, communication advice, how to overcome shyness, etc.

59.The majority of people desire safety in their lives and environments. They desire to keep themselves and their loved ones safe from harm or threats from others. You may focus on specialized goods like CPR instruction, local risks information, home safety supplies, etc.

60.Many people prefer to appear younger or older than they actually are. You might focus on specialized goods like anti-aging products, cosmetics, attire, disguises, etc.

61.Receiving Praise - Most people desire to receive compliments, praise, and congratulations for their achievements. You might focus on specialized goods and services like coaching for public speaking, career guidance, and self-improvement programs.

62.Convenience - The majority of individuals desire convenience. You might focus on specialist goods like quick and simple meal planning tools, labor-saving ways and services, etc.

63.The majority of people desire to be understood. You might focus on specialized goods and services like speech audios, grammatical guides, communication strategies, and other topics.

64.Being environmentally conscious - A lot of consumers prefer products that are eco-friendly. You might focus on environmentally friendly specialized goods and services, such as cleaning supplies, chemicals, air fresheners, automobiles, insecticides, etc.

65. Avoiding Waste - A lot of individuals choose recyclable packaging or goods. You might focus on specialized goods and services like those that recycle metals, plastics, paper, cans, and other materials.

66.Belonging To Groups - Many people aspire to be a part of a certain social group. You might focus on specialized goods and services for groups like sports teams, clubs, associations, get-togethers, and seminars.

67.The majority of people wish to complete a particular activity or task. You may focus on providing specialized goods and services like guidance on action, goal-setting, and following through.

68.Changing Someone - Many people wish they could influence the opinions of others. They are attempting to avoid anything that might interfere with their own personal objectives. You could focus on specialized goods or services, such as those related to public speaking, influence and persuasion strategies, copywriting, marketing, and nonverbal communication.

69.Being an Authority Figure - Many people aspire to be leaders. You might concentrate on providing specialized goods and services, such as parent education courses and professional leadership training seminars.

70.The majority of individuals desire features that will both make their lives easier and provide benefits. Gaining Benefits/Feature You might focus on specialist goods and services like add-ons to a standard product, such as free pick-up and delivery, service plans, free shipping, etc.

71.The majority of people wish to find solutions to their difficulties, solving Problems you could concentrate on specialized goods and solutions like problem-solving abilities, Getting through barriers, handling (a particular issue), etc.

72.Breaking a Negative Habit - Many people seek to get rid of their bad behaviors. You may focus on specialized goods and services, such as those that help people stop overeating, stop biting their nails, or stop smoking.

73.Developing Good Habits – Developing good habits for oneself is a goal for many people. You might concentrate on providing specialized goods and services like advice on healthy nutrition, exercise, and rest.

74.Getting An Advantage The desire to outperform others or circumstance is shared by many people. You might concentrate on offering specialized advice, techniques, methods, and other services.

75.Thinking positively is something that plenty of individuals aspire to do. You might focus on specialized goods and services like advice on how to think positively, etc. Most people wish to alter some aspect of their surroundings, which brings us to point

76. You might concentrate on providing specialized goods and services, such as decorating ideas, books on home renovation, gardening advice, etc.

77.Most people wish to change something about themselves. You might go for specialized goods and services like self-help, fashionable attire, cosmetics, exercise gear, etc.

78.Having natural products is a popular preference among consumers. You could concentrate on providing specialist goods and services like all-natural snacks, drinks, cleaning products, and cuisine.

79.Smile and Be Joyful - Most people want to smile and laugh. Such products and services as humor, jokes, greeting cards, etc. could be your niche market.

80.Gaining Weight - Some individuals seek to increase their body weight. You may focus on specialized goods and services, such as protein drinks, equipment for working out, and muscle-building supplements.

81.The majority of people desire a sense of security. Being uneasy, exposed, or even feeling unsafe is something they wish to avoid. You might concentrate on providing specialized goods and services such as secure ordering, credit card security measures, locks, security systems, and safety equipment.

82.Being Generous - Generosity and giving are traits that many individuals possess. You might concentrate on providing specialized goods and services, such as presents, donations, non-profit services, and auctions for good causes.

83.Being at ease is a desire shared by the majority of people. Like cozy clothing, seat cushions, velvet blankets, etc., you might focus on specialized goods and services.

84.Having Morality and Ethics - Most people have morality and ethics. You could focus on specialized goods and services like religious goods, parental control devices, parental rating systems, business standards, and things related to the law and the legal system.

85.Support - Most people prefer to have other people back them up in the positions they take. Confrontations are something they desire to avoid. You may choose to target specialized goods and services like those provided by lawyers, accountants, bodyguards, and providers of defensive gear, among others.

86.Peace of Mind - Most people prefer to live solitary lifestyles. You may concentrate on specialized goods and services, such as those that guard against identity theft, promote privacy, or include blinds and tinted windows.

87.Able to Provide Assistance - Most people are kind, considerate, and sympathetic. They don't want an issue or catastrophe to cause others to struggle. You may choose to target specialized goods and services like charitable organizations and volunteer work.

88.Being Challenged – People enjoy challenges. When presented with challenges, people want to demonstrate that they are capable of overcoming them. Real-world television, pie eating competitions, and other specialty products and services could be your focus.

89.Having a Spirit of Adventure - Many people are seeking for an adventure. Like extreme sports, adventurous travel, bungee jumping, parachuting, etc., you could focus on specialist products and services.

90.Scam Avoidance - Nobody wants to fall victim to a scam. You might focus on specialized goods and solutions like reviews of products, services, and legitimate business opportunities, as well as services that report scams.

91.Having a Calm Attitude - Most people want to live a calm, unhurried existence. They don't want to feel pressured, anxious, worried, or tense. Such specialized goods and services as vacations, hypnosis, message theory, etc.

92.Being Terrified - A lot of people take amusingly being terrified quite seriously. Such specialized goods and services as spooky movies, haunted attractions, Halloween garb, etc.

93.Being Competitive - Many individuals enjoy competition. Sports, video games, competitive events, and other specialist markets are possible to target.

94.Being Confident: The majority of individuals enjoy having confidence. You might market specialized goods and services, such as advice on boosting self-assurance, ways to improve self-esteem, strenuous activities, etc.

95.Most people like to smell well, thus this is number you might target specialty goods and services like deodorant, cologne, perfume, air fresheners, and breath fresheners, among others.

96.Being Wired/Unwired – A lot of people desire a global connection. They do not want to overlook an opportunity or neglect to communicate with important persons in their lives. You might concentrate on certain items like Internet access, video conferencing, satellite television, cable, mobile phones, laptop computers, Internet cafes, etc.

97.Child Supporting - There are many folks that need to provide for their children. You might concentrate on specialized goods like children's apparel, toys, games, kid-friendly foods, infant products, etc.

98.Being Well-Groomed - The majority of people desire to be well-groomed. Products like electronic groomers, razors, shaving cream, finger nail polish, hair spray, nose hair cutters, and hair salons are examples of specialized goods that you could target.

99.Being Well-Clothed: The majority of people aim to dress nicely or wear certain things. You might focus on specialized goods and services like apparel, fashion design, uniforms, sewing machines, and publications for the clothing industry.

Bonus Material:

100.Giving Back to the Community - There is always a need to give back to the community. Look for an area where you have expertise and volunteer to help. Once your knowledge is acknowledged even nationally, the service will be valued and you may be able to identify a void to fill for a profit. A great place to start is in your neighborhood.

ABOUT THE AUTHOR

Annabelle Jeffrey is a relentless worker with a clear sense of purpose who finds potential in everything, no matter what the circumstances. She holds that you should try rising again no matter how many times you fall.

www.ingramcontent.com/pod-product-compliance
Lightning Source LLC
LaVergne TN
LVHW020543160826
845677LV00015B/4171

9798355353377